# Customer Service

Perspectives and Considerations

for the

EMS Leader

John R. Brophy

Copyright © 2015 John R. Brophy

All rights reserved.

ISBN: 1505678161
ISBN-13: 978-1505678161

# A TRIBUTE

In my previous four books I included a Dedication and had a trusted colleague write a Forward as part of the finishing touches to the project.

In this case I am opting for a change of pace. Today I would like to put forth A Tribute in their stead. I am doing so because at the time of my final edits the EMS world lost a tremendous leader and I lost a treasured friend and valued mentor.

Cheryl Delikat was an EMS Supervisor in Jersey City, New Jersey. In life she epitomized dedication, excellence, and most of all compassion for both her coworkers and patients alike. When she passed it was in the memories that were eulogized that I believe we all found strength.

When I left Jersey City to pursue my career I was Cheryl's boss. I say that not to brag on myself, but rather to reinforce what a mentor and leader she was. I started as a per-diem field employee and eventually found my way to a full-time position on Cheryl's team in the communications center. In retrospect I truly believe that my career and life were greatly enhanced as a result. There were four of us on her team at the time and every one of us went on to become Supervisors. Cheryl had a unique way of bringing the best out of people. She developed her people through her passion for excellence.

But I don't just write this tribute because of the timing or because I somehow regret not having said these things to her in words and deeds over the years. I did all those things. In fact I recall my final leadership team meeting in Jersey City. We had a guest speaker, Dr. Frank Mineo, who asked the group to talk about mentors we have had. I immediately told the story about how Cheryl had not only groomed me to become her boss, but that everyone on our team had gone onto become supervisors.

To me Cheryl was the ultimate mentor and team builder. She deserved the kudos among her peers and superiors alike. I have consulted with her and she with me since leaving Jersey City on a variety of issues. I write this tribute because at the core of her being Cheryl taught us the importance of the patient as a person. Everything she taught us was centered on the simple truth that patients are people first.

Thanks for the memories Cheryl. Your legacy lives on in everything we do.

# CONTENTS

|  | Acknowledgments | i |
|---|---|---|
|  | Preface | iii |
| 1 | Doctor am I going to die? | 1 |
| 2 | General Impression | 3 |
| 3 | Wrinkle City & Fossil Farms | 7 |
| 4 | Is courtesy a priority? | 9 |
| 5 | Modeling the way | 13 |
| 6 | Follow-up | 19 |
| 7 | One Customer's Experiences | 25 |
| 8 | Comfort of the Ride | 33 |
| 9 | Transfer OTP | 37 |
| 10 | 9-1-1 OTP | 43 |
| 11 | Service Excellence Metrics | 47 |

| | | |
|---|---|---|
| 12 | Perception – A Case Study | 51 |
| 13 | Verbalization – Not Just for Testing Anymore | 55 |
| 14 | The Toe Truck | 57 |
| 15 | Bridge Trolls & Negative Influences | 59 |
| 16 | Patch up Your House | 63 |
| 17 | He's My Dad | 67 |
| 18 | Invest in Customer Service | 71 |
| 19 | Nice Matters | 75 |
| 20 | Essentials of Customer Service in EMS | 79 |
| | References | 83 |
| | About the Author | 87 |
| | Other Titles by John R. Brophy | 89 |

# ACKNOWLEDGMENTS

As I put the finishing touches on this my fifth book I can't help but reflect upon everyone in my life and career that has had an impact on me.

Over the past 30 plus years I have been blessed with a career that matters. One that has allowed me to touch the lives of so many patients and their families, both directly as a care giver and indirectly as an instructor and leader.

Every encounter has provided opportunities, both positive and negative, for me to learn and grow as a professional and a person.

It would be impossible for me to adequately list everyone who has contributed individually to my ability to put together my thoughts and perspectives on customer service as it relates to EMS. So today I simply want to acknowledge everyone who has touched my life thus far for the influence you have had that has allowed me to succeed.

My hope is that their collective influence has allowed me to become a better provider, leader, and person. One who has parlayed their investments in me in a way that has impacted the world in a positive way.

# PREFACE

When someone calls or needs an ambulance it is a significant event. Think about it, how often have you needed an ambulance as a patient? Depending on where we work we go on dozens, hundreds, even thousands of ambulance calls a year. But each response may be the first time a patient ever needed an ambulance. Until that moment they have been able to navigate life without the need for our help. As a result each patient is going through a variety of thoughts and emotions - fear of the unknown, concern for themselves and their families, even embarrassment for some. And that is just the first time and infrequent emergency users of EMS.

What about the frequent users? The ones often stigmatized by their situations and repeated use of ours and other services. With the exception of the critically ill or injured these are perhaps the ones in most need of our services – and the services of others. Their lives have spiraled, slowly or rapidly to a point where they have the need – actual or perceived – to call 9-1-1. Sometimes they need acute medical attention, sometimes not. But each time they need our compassion and human interaction to help them through their most recent dark moment.

Let's not forget the inter-facility transfer patients and those we take to dialysis and other treatments on a regular basis. These patients and their families rely upon us to get them where they need to go when they need to be there. They need us because an ambulance is the only safe way for them to get there. But it is far more than, as I have often heard it, "you call – we'll haul". They need more than just the logistics we provide in getting them from point A to point B. They need us to be understanding, friendly, and kind.

No matter the reason for the call, the patient has a need, be it actual or perceived. In our training we focus a lot on the time-life-critical skills and rightfully so. In this book we will focus on the whole patient, their families, and others who rely on us to provide them with customer service every day.

# 1 DOCTOR AM I GOING TO DIE?

This is a question a patient of mine asked her doctor. It was way back in the early 1980's. I was working for a small, family owned, ambulance company at the time. My partner and I responded to a call for an older female that was ill. She lived in a high-rise building and as fate would have it, so too did her semi-retired physician.

When we arrived he was in her apartment with her. He provided us a history and his diagnosis of her current situation. We assisted her onto the stretcher and were ready to head for the hospital. At this point she asked her doctor to accompany her. He agreed.

In the ambulance the doctor and I were in back with her. A few minutes into the ride she said "Doctor, am I going to die?" He reached out and gently, but firmly held her hand. Without a moment's hesitation he replied "Dying is the last thing you are going to do." She smiled and the sense of her more relaxed state was palpable.

Some 30 years later I still remember that encounter. Why? My guess is because it was simple, yet profound. He was 100% truthful – dying is the last thing every one of us will do. But at the same time what he said was meant to be reassuring and put her as much at ease as he could in the situation. It was people care more so than patient care. For me it was an invaluable lesson. One I had the opportunity to learn very early in my career. One I have shared countless times in conversations, coaching sessions, and classes over the years. One which I share today to memorialize it in the hopes even more people can benefit from what I consider the timeless wisdom of this doctor.

What I learned was treat the whole person, not just the patient and their symptoms. Many years later I had the opportunity to not only watch the movie *Patch Adams*, but read the book *Gesundheit* (Adams & Mylander, 1998). In it we are reminded that all of us are humans and as such inhabit our own stories – the historic traditions that make each of us unique, not just a "case". The movie and the book, along with all of my patient encounters along the way reinforced for me just how important that simple lesson from the "old school" doctor was for me. It also reminded me just how important it is that I continue to share it with all who will take the time to listen.

While seeing the encounter live was quite impactful, I hope you will take away the message in your own way and apply it to your practice of pre-hospital care.

# 2 GENERAL IMPRESSION

If general impression were a roadway, it would be a two way street.

We are taught to quickly assess safety, overall patient condition, the environment and a whole lot more in the first few seconds of each patient encounter. Reality is that the patients, their families, and the public all have a similar skillset when it comes to us. The only difference is they were never told there is a name for it.

They judge us on and off calls. They form a general impression of our response times, the cleanliness of our uniforms and ambulances, whether or not we show enough interest and compassion for their situation, and a whole lot more. They have a vision of what we should be. Sometimes it is a fair one, sometimes one we may believe to be unrealistic. No matter their view, they are entitled to it and we are put into a position in which we must live up to it every time we put on the uniform.

It is a rainy slippery day and you are called to a high school football field for a player with an ankle injury. You respond without lights and sirens because the risk outweighs the benefit of getting there a minute or so sooner. Upon arrival you make your way onto the field with you equipment. At patient side you find the trainer who has already splinted the player so you load him on the stretcher and head back off the field.

The next day your boss gets a call from a city councilman. They say their office was flooded with calls that EMS took too long and "meandered on and off the field with no sense of urgency whatsoever".

As the crew what would your thoughts be?

What about if you are the manager? How do you proceed?

Could this complaint have been prevented?

Can it be used as an opportunity to improve customer perceptions?

The reality is that operationally and clinically everything was done right. But that is our reality, what about theirs? The councilman and his constituents perceive we took too long and showed no urgency. The lesson is that we can provide proper service but still fall short of expectations.

In his book *Hey, I'm the Customer* Ron Willingham (1992) tells a story of going into a gift shop shortly before closing time. He was greeted by a sales associate and her first words were "We close in fifteen minutes!"

What message did she send? To me (and from reading his book, to Ron as well) the message was "be sure to hurry up so I don't have to stay late to ring up your purchase". Did she even realize how what she said could have been perceived negatively? Was her comment truly innocuous or was she actually expressing true frustration with a customer coming in so close to closing?

Now let's change the scenario from a gift shop back to EMS. It is 15 minutes before shift change and you are sent on a non-life threatening call - so much for getting out on time. Will your disappointment come across in your interactions with this patient and their loved ones?

These are the challenges we face every day in EMS. While both are different, both are the same. They both involve how we portray ourselves and how we are perceived by the people we serve. Some may say we are judged against an unfair set of subjective standards and they wouldn't be entirely wrong. In the final analysis however, as EMS professionals we must adjust to the field upon which we play.

# 3 WRINKLE CITY & FOSSIL FARMS

These were terms some used to describe the two senior housing complexes in the community where I cut my teeth as a volunteer EMT. Creative? Yes, yet inappropriate and obnoxious at the same time. Fortunately for me I grew up with many older family members who reinforced the importance of respect for my elders. But then, didn't most of us? One would hope.

I think the tipping point came with how some of the senior members of the ambulance corps handled some of the calls I was on at Wrinkle City and Fossil Farms. In fact two patients in particular come to mind. They were sisters with their own apartments in the same senior building. Whenever they would have a fight, which would be about once or twice a month, one or both would call us. We would respond, calm them down, and obtain a signed refusal of transport.

What came next was that my mentors would then call us back in service, but we would stay and have a cup of coffee or tea with one or both of them. The service they needed was not for some life threatening condition. They needed someone to listen. And we were there.

Some might call that system abuse. I would disagree. EMS exists to provide care to those in need. We provided care. We listened and we helped them through their difficult times when they had no one else they could call.

People are at the center of what we do. They call us when they have a need, perceived or actual. It is what we signed up for. The problem is that often our recruiters, instructors and even our leaders painted a different picture for us. They sold us a bill of goods that it would be all lights and sirens as we snatched life from the clutches of death.

In fairness, I guess at times I was guilty of the sales pitch myself. In fact I challenge anyone in EMS to honestly say they didn't either sell the pitch, buy it – or both. In retrospect however, I think I have gained a large portion of my people centered focus from these early experiences with wise mentors like Sy, Janet, Gloria, Barbara, Harold, Pam and Cathi. They helped me build my skills as a provider and leader very early on in my now 30 year and counting career. Mostly though, they taught me the importance of the "care" part of patient care.

# 4 IS COURTESY A PRIORITY?

We all know safety comes first, but what's next and were is courtesy on the list? It is like the ABC's of Customer Service. And if you think about it, for years Airway always was first, then, Breathing, and then Circulation – then a few years back we switched from ABC to CAB. Why? Because we found doing so had better results.

What are your service priorities after safety? Are they what they should be? Are they in the right order? Does everyone in your organization know the order?

Starting with the last question first, let's assume you have your key priorities and they are in an order you are comfortable with. It is important that the people in the organization know the priorities so that when faced with a choice they can make an informed decision.

Disney's priorities are Safety, Courtesy, The Show, and then Efficiency. Banks may put accuracy above responsiveness while a hotel will likely flip the order of these two priorities. In healthcare we are all in sync that safety comes first, but how often do we put efficiency before our employees and even our patients?

In some cases too often and why is that? I think it is because our service priorities are not clear.

We post units on street corners to shorten response times and press our crews to get back in service quickly after dropping off their patients. The results accomplish shorter response times and higher utilization (more efficient). But the cost is fatigued and stressed out crews expected to put on a good show (courteous, professional, and clinically competent care). Shaving seconds and saving a few bucks but what is the real cost? Crews get there quick, rush through the call, then move onto the next one. If this sounds like your organization or one you know, my guess is that either there isn't a pecking order for the service standards or there aren't any.

Service standards are separate from values. The organizational values are its moral compass, while the service standards are the rules of engagement for providing customer service (Snow & Yantovitch, 2003). So, to put it in EMS terms, Values are our overall Strategy and Service Standards are our Customer Service Tactics.

So as you walk away from this chapter it would be a good idea to evaluate or create a set of Customer Service Standards. Be sure they support your organization's Values. Seek wide input and feedback, then be sure to publish the final product so everyone knows them. Doing so will empower your people to be consistent in their approach by providing them with the information needed make a good decision when faced with a choice of customer service activities.

# 5 MODELING THE WAY

It has both been said and proven that people in organizations will pay attention to what their leaders pay attention to. They will also pay as much, if not more attention to what you do as what you say. If you come in late a lot, your uniform or business attire is unkept, or your actions don't match your expectations for your people they will notice. They will also lose respect for what you preach because you are not practicing it.

The leader also needs to be the coach, mentor, & guide. The leader must be ready, willing and able to recognize and address opportunities that present themselves in a way that will support the employee and guide them in improving their performance.

Let's look at a case study...

Among an EMS supervisors tasks for their next shift is to issue a write-up for an employee exceeding the allowable number of tardy occurrences to a member of their team. If this write-up came as a surprise to either the supervisor or the employee then we have a failure of leadership. That's right this write-up may not entirely be the fault of the employee. Hold on, you say...if the employee shows up late how is that the supervisor's fault?

Ultimately you are correct in your knee-jerk – the employee is ultimately responsible for their own behavior. But consider this. Had the supervisor noticed the employee being tardy more frequently than the once or twice a year that "stuff" inevitably happens the supervisor may have had an opportunity to intervene. Instead they went about their day and did not notice nor react to the tardiness of the employee. They were not paying attention, so the employee didn't either. In fact it is entirely possible the employee thought nothing of it because they saw the supervisor every day as they punched in late and not a word was said about it. The later, represents the supervisor's missing an opportunity to coach or mentor. The end result, an employee who received punishment for something they perceived by the supervisor's inattention as being ok.

So why do I bring this up in a book about customer service? It's simple...as leaders our people are our customers too. The reality is that customer relations simply mirror employee relations (Peters & Waterman, 2004). If leaders don't pay attention to things that are important to and for their people they cannot expect their people to magically do the things their leaders don't.

Perhaps if the supervisor had engaged the employee earlier on about the habitual tardiness the write-up would never have occurred, perhaps in talking with the employee they may have found that something in the employee's life had changed and could have facilitated a shift transfer to a more amenable schedule – in other words some form of truly corrective action. Not just issuing a "punishment" form that calls itself "corrective action" and is filed away. Again, as leaders we reap what we sow. The better we take care of our people the better they will take care of our customers.

By modeling the way and treating our people with respect, dignity, and empathy we will be providing them both the positive examples they need and the environment in which these behaviors can be replicated.

Another aspect of leadership as it relates to customer service is the approach of senior leadership. Dinah Nemeroff of Citibank did a study in 1980. She calls it "Service Statesmanship", which senior leaders exercise through personal example. In her study she found that the effectiveness of their close-to-the-customer-through-service concept was effective because top managers treated service problems as "real time" issues – issues that deserve their immediate personal attention. She went onto discuss how the executives involved in this top management style believed they must maintain a long-term view of service as a revenue builder (Peters & Waterman, 2004). In the final analysis, her research reinforces that leaders at all levels can and must take a personal stake in customer relations every day for an organization to provide the best service they can.

I recall a complaint I received from the family member of a dialysis patient. They said that the ambulance is always late picking their loved one up after their treatment is finished. I apologized that we had not met their expectations and asked them to allow me the opportunity to look into the situation.

We all know how it sometimes goes. Something happens twice and the perception of the customer is that "it happens all the time". Well, remember the old adage "fool me once shame on you, fool me twice shame on me". Well from the customer's perspective after being "fooled twice" they may start losing confidence in our ability to provide quality on-time service. This in turn could result in their seeking out another provider who will "wow", not "fool" them.

When I dug into the complaint I started by looking at what time we had been picking the patient up every day. I compared this to our service excellence standard of a 30 minute response time on all unscheduled non-emergency calls. I found over a period of about 4 weeks we had only missed the 30 minute mark once. I also noticed that we were receiving the call that the patient was ready within about the same 5 to 10 minute window just about every time.

Until that complaint anywhere I had ever worked in the ambulance industry the system was the same on dialysis patients. Schedule the outgoing pick-up and wait for the call to tell us the patient was ready. Then send the return ambulance. Why not try something different? As Einstein was renowned for saying insanity is doing the same thing over and over and expecting a different result.

Insane no more, I thought about different ways to change what we were doing to achieve a different, better result. It was as simple as it was creative. We pre-scheduled the returns. I am sure about now some of you are saying "duh" and others are saying "wow we have to try that". No matter your response, the reality is that it worked.

We first tried it with the initial patient whose family raised concerns. Once we found it to be more effective we rolled it out to almost all of our round-trip patients. I say almost all, because some were not as predictable or consistent as most with their ready times.

When I called back the family and explained our findings and our plan they were appreciative, but sounded a bit skeptical. Perhaps because they thought "well if it is so simple to fix why didn't you do it that way all along". Can't say I had a good answer for that thought, but we agreed to give it a try and keep track of it. For the next week I made a point of monitoring every day. I also told dispatch staff to let me know ahead of time if they thought we would be late for this patient. Their concerns were both individually important and if we were able to manage this new approach well with this patient we could apply it to others and improve the service they receive as well.

We achieved success because we listened and took this customer's concerns seriously. Listening to our customers, be they internal or external is a critical element of leadership. Unfortunately there are too many published stories about companies that thought they knew better. One example is when customers demanded small, reliable cars with good mileage. Detroit thought otherwise and lost 30 percent of the marketplace (Lynch & Cross, 1994). Take the time to listen and then act on what you are hearing.

Ultimately the leader's role in customer service is to model the way.

# 6 FOLLOW-UP

How quickly does your agency respond to a call reporting a lost article - clothing, a watch, an insurance ID card? Does that call take on a sense of urgency or is it one of those low priorities that will maybe find its way to some superficial attention?

Have you ever heard the adage "one man's trash is another man's treasure"? It generally relates to used items at garage sales and flea markets. Stuff someone no longer wants or needs (trash) is often just the thing (treasure) someone else wants or needs. But sometimes by our actions we connect it to a call of this nature. "It's only an insurance ID card, they can just call their insurance company or go on line and get another one" is but one of the many comments I have heard about patient belongings over the years. Their treasure has become our trash!

Handling this type of call is something rental car companies and EMS have in common. People in vehicles other than their own often leave things behind. In these cases the most crucial person in the recovery effort is the person who takes the call (Kazanjian, 2013). Empathy is key.

Granted these calls should not rank higher than a 9-1-1 call, but I would argue they are deserving of a response by the end of the day. Even if the initial response is just to acknowledge the call while you check with crew's, have someone go look in the ambulance they were transported in, check the PCR for any notations concerning belongings, or find them the direct number to the person they need to speak with at the facility they were transported to – the important thing is to listen first and express genuine concern.

Next is the need to actually do what you promised. If you said you would have someone go check the ambulance – have someone go check the ambulance. Then, no matter the findings, call them back and give them closure. It has been proven that the return on investment from such phone calls is huge in terms of the goodwill created and loyalty captured (Zemke & Bell, 2003). Will this take a little of our time? Time we all know is precious and often scarce in EMS leadership. Absolutely, but it is not time you are spending – it is time you are investing. Investing in the people that you serve who, in-turn will reinvest it in your organization when they think and talk about their experience with you.

Another area of follow-up is regarding surveys. If yours is an organization that invests in sending out a satisfaction survey it is important that you take the good with the bad. For certain you need to tout the positives with your internal and external stakeholders.

But what about the responses that paint a less than flattering picture of the service they received?

The sad reality is that research in the health care field has found that some patients keep quiet for fear of retaliation until after they are discharged. According to Zemke & Bell (2003) following up with a phone call or survey gives an organization a second chance to resolve the customer's problem, and potentially win back their trust and loyalty.

So when that survey comes back or that phone call comes in with a bad review it is providing a second chance to make things right. The concern may be an actual shortcoming or simply a perception. Either way, in the eyes of this client the organization has already failed. The caveat is that they are reaching out and giving us a chance to make things right. Often times this involves nothing more than an acknowledgement that we didn't meet "their" expectations – even if we did everything clinically and operationally correct. Sometimes it involves a conversation about perception with a crew, which will hopefully provide them a teachable moment they can apply going forward. Still others may involve something more serious requiring different actions.

I recall a time when I processed a few complaints and forwarded them to the person responsible for their follow-up. The result was a "spirited" discussion between us. They told me that the information I provided sounded "accusatory". We discussed the fact that complaints often are accusatory among other things. He had a complaint about the complaints. We heard each other out. In the end we agreed that accusatory or not we can't "shoot the messenger" if we are to get the most benefit out of any complaints we receive. Whether or not the complaint is ultimately determined to be valid it is important to listen past the "motives" of the caller. Just because they may be trying to get us to waive a bill or issue a refund does not automatically mean their complaint is invalid. We need to put cynicism aside and determine what we can gain from their complaint.

I don't blindly subscribe to the "customer is always right". But one thing is certain; the customer is always the customer. As such, we owe it to them and to our organization and industry to listen and take action accordingly. A study published by the White House in 1981 found that 70% of the people who complained about a company and were satisfied with their response remained more loyal to the company than if they had not complained, and they told their friends about their positive experience (Yellin, 2009). They gave us a "do-over". As kids we would sometimes use it as a means of amicably settling a disagreement in something we were doing. Maybe as kids we were onto something with the "do-over". A simple acknowledgement that sometimes we are wrong and many times we can do better can go a long way toward improving both performance and customer service.

In the final analysis, whether it is a lost article, a complaint, or a request for follow-up for any other reason we owe it to our clients as well as our organizations to do our best to listen and respond with empathy in a timely manner.

Mistakes happen, but genuine and timely follow-up matters.

# 7 ONE CUSTOMER'S EXPERIENCES

Let me tell a story of two polar opposite customer service encounters I had when calling "customer service". And while I am the "One Customer" to which this chapter refers, I know from conversations with friends and strangers alike that my experience is not uncommon.

So, shortly after moving into a new home I had the opportunity to contact a credit card company to do my change of address. Sometimes companies have a space to fill out on the bill for a change of address and then just send it in – not in this case. So I looked over the bill and found the "customer service" number. I made the call, was greeted with the automated request for what the purpose of my call was – mine of course was not one of the selections. After repeating the word "representative" multiple times I was asked for my account number so my call could be properly routed. I punched it in, heard a ring and then got a message that my "anticipated wait time would be 7 minutes". So I put the phone on speaker and moved onto something else while I was waiting.

A few minutes later, I didn't pay attention to how accurate the 7 minute estimate was, a "representative" came on the line, gave their name asked for mine. I introduced myself. They then asked me for my account number. Wait a minute, didn't I punch that in? I told them I punched it in and asked why they needed it again. They simply said they needed it before we could proceed. So I rattled it off – again! They then asked how they could help me and I said I simply needed to do a change of address. Wait for it.... They replied that I called the wrong 800 number. Before I had a chance to reply they rattled it off, without even first asking if I was ready to copy it down. When I asked why they couldn't assist me they said "I am in customer service and we don't do that here."

I took a deep breath. Held back what first came to mind and asked them to repeat the other number for me. They then ended the call by asking me if there was anything else they could help me with. Really?

So I called the other number and received a recording, in the same voice as the previous automated system, saying "your estimated hold time is 7 minutes". Hmmm, where had I heard that before? It made me think of the take out places that when you call in an order, no matter its size or complexity, they tell you it will be ready in 20 minutes.

Since I had a credit balance on my card due to a recent return, I hung-up in frustration thinking "Send the bill wherever you want, I don't owe you anything anyway!"

So why am I writing about this in a book about EMS customer service? It is to illustrate the point that somehow and some way the credit card company protocols were adopted to address my situation and countless others. On the back-end they are probably pretty efficient for their workload. What about the perspective of the customer? This representative and the system worked precisely as designed, yet my needs would only have been met if I chose to endure another 7 minute hold. Think about some of our protocols and how they might be perceived by the public, even though they make perfect sense to us.

Take the Medical Priority Dispatch System (MPDS) for example. It is designed to ask key questions to determine acuity of the patient's condition and then send the most appropriate response. Sometimes call takers are met with similar frustrations to what I just described. To them, asking a few questions is sometimes akin to my 7 minute hold. What about when they have a low-acuity situation that to them is "urgent". We opt for safety and send a unit without lights and sirens and they complain that we took too long. Our process is designed for safety, but to them it is but another "7 minute hold" experience when we take longer than they expected to answer "their call".

Our systems are set-up for crew and public safety balanced against the time-life critical and non-time-life critical needs of those who request our service. It probably doesn't take a scientifically conducted public opinion poll to find evidence of the contempt most Americans harbor toward bad customer service or to elicit testimony about the effects of that kind of antipathy in their lives (Yellin, 2009). In retrospect, my frustration of being triaged the equivalent of an EMS Omega call by my credit card company because they prioritized other customer needs like reporting lost or stolen cards, payments and disputes of charges to be higher acuity was eye opening. I felt I received poor customer service, but their system simply put people with more pressing needs ahead of me. No matter how they justify it and explain the rationale, it was still a negative customer experience for me. Their objective system did not meet my subjective needs.

The question is, can we in EMS operate an objective system in an environment of subjective consumers of our services without coming up short over and over again? I think so. Let's look at a different customer experience I had, this time with L.L. Bean.

For those who don't know L.L. Bean is a retailer with both stores and catalog/on-line distribution of their products. They have been in business for over 100 years, starting with one store in 1912 and a guarantee. Here is their approach... "Our guarantee is based on something as simple as a handshake – the deal that you'll be satisfied with a purchase, and if you are not, we'll make it right. We guarantee that we'll hold up our end of the bargain. It's just how we do business. If your purchase isn't completely satisfactory, we're happy to accept your exchange or return at any time."

So it was the holiday season a year ago. I ordered a few items from L.L. Bean. Some gifts, some personal items. When they arrived one of the items was the wrong color. So I called L.L. Bean customer service. When I did I was greeted with a human being on the other end of the line. I explained what happened. They immediately took responsibility and apologized for not meeting my expectations. No attempt to transfer me or to figure out a way that I had somehow placed the order wrong. In a word, wow!

The representative immediately asked if it was a gift for the holidays. She even offered to have it gift wrapped and shipped anywhere I needed it to be so that I was not further inconvenienced. Beyond wow!

Next she assured me the item would ship the same day express delivery at no charge to me. The only quid pro quo she had for me was that I hold onto the incorrect item until a return label was received and ship it back. I actually felt guilty having that being my only responsibility. What a difference between L.L. Bean customer service and my credit card company.

I had a simple one item error and it was as important to them as a $10,000 order – at least in my perspective. In his book *L.L. Bean - The Making of an American Icon* by Leon Gorman (2006), the grandson of L.L. Bean wrote we wanted activist telephone reps and support staff who fully engaged with customers' questions and who made sure we responded. Well from my experience they got what they wanted. They were walking the talk for sure!

Relating this second experience back to EMS they took my comparatively low acuity one-item return and recognized that while it was not a big deal to their overall multi-million dollar operation it was important to me. I was treated with respect and dignity. My needs were not just met, but exceeded. They remembered that I wasn't just a number, but that there was a person behind the incorrect order. Their genuine concern shined through. So even when we go no lights and sirens to that "minor" injury call, we can and must remember that they called us because it is a big deal to them. We need to treat the person, not just the injury. The L.L. Bean rep did that for me. They easily could have mechanically walked through the return process without empathy or concern. Instead the empathy and concern was central to the encounter and the return was handled, but almost secondary to making sure my human needs were cared for.

So, Echo, Omega, or anywhere between, remember every call involves at least one person besides us. It's their world, we just work in it. Take care of their injuries and illnesses, but always treat the whole person.

# 8 COMFORT OF THE RIDE

So we respond to an emergency or even a transfer call. We do our assessment, perform any necessary treatments and move the patient onto our stretcher and away we go. Sounds like a typical day in EMS right?

I have a cousin who is in the Merchant Marine. He has had many years of opportunities to travel the world. As often happens when people travel the world they bring back souvenirs for themselves or others close to them. I remember one such time early in my cousin's Merchant Marine career when he brought me back a shot glass from one of his ports of call. I had picked him up from the airport and when we got home he reached into his carry-on to give me this gift. When he did his hand came back out of the bag with a cut on it, a cut from the shot glass that had broken during the trip because it was not properly packaged. Best intentions for sure, but poor execution. Both my gift and my cousin were damaged in the process.

The shot glass and my cousin's finger are metaphors for our patients and for us. If we don't properly package them for transport they will suffer ill effects. Granted the ill effects need not be an injury, but they could be a patient who is too hot or too cold or one that simply could have used a pillow to improve their ride. This also may result in a patient or their family that is left with a poor impression of the quality of our care.

Thom Dick is a consummate and passionate advocate of patients and their caregivers. He has decades of experience in EMS. In 2005 he, along with Steve Berry, Jeff Forster, and Mike Smith wrote a book called *People Care*. It includes lots of great insights and I believe it is a must read for everyone in EMS. In it there is a chapter called Ceiling Inspections.

In Ceiling Inspections they talk about the importance of providing a perspective for providers as to what a patient will experience when riding in an ambulance and looking at the ceiling. It talks about having EMT's and Paramedics take a ride on the stretcher in various states of dress – swimsuit vs. uniform for example. Also various states of other things like with a blanket and without, on a backboard, and with or without a pillow were discussed. Their point being perhaps we need to do more to walk a mile in the shoes of our patients so we can better understand what is important to them and why.

Fortunately for most in EMS filling the role of patient on a call is foreign. It is a blessing and a curse. A blessing for the obvious reasons that by and large we haven't needed the services we provide. But a curse in that we don't have the first hand perspective that might help us be a better people-centered provider.

In over 30 years in the industry I had but one occasion to be a patient in an ambulance. I was injured in my role as a firefighter (3 broken ribs) was transported by ambulance to the hospital. I was not critical; in fact I walked to the ambulance. But the ride, well that was another story all together. The pain was not excruciating or anything, but during the eight or so mile trip I did feel as if I was experiencing every crack, crevice, and pothole between the fire scene and the hospital. Given the pre-existing relationships the crew was comfortable with me and I with them. As such the interpersonal communication was excellent. They offered what they could in the way of comfort measures and were empathetic throughout. With the exception of making me laugh a couple of times – which hurt more than the cracks in the road – everything they did was focused on my comfort.

The result, a satisfied customer who experienced an uncomfortable ride but knew then and now that everything humanly possible to make me comfortable was done. I knew it was going to hurt and so did they. We communicated and worked through it together. I even recall seeing a wince or two from the crew on some of the bumps – empathy winces for sure as I know from sitting where they were thousands of times that there was no actual pain for them. I knew they cared and that made a huge difference in my patient perspective of the encounter.

The takeaway here is that even when there are things we can't do much about, doing what we can and showing that we care will take the edge off and ultimately result in a better patient experience.

# 9 TRANSFER OTP

I recall a meeting a colleague and I were going to attend on the subject of on-time performance (OTP). It was with one of our larger clients and only about 15 or so minutes from our office. When I told the colleague what time I wanted to leave (an hour before the scheduled time of the meeting) she said "you do know they are only about 5 miles from here right?" I said "yes I do, but I am not going to be the guy walking in late to a meeting about being on time." We both got a chuckle, but agreed that early is generally better anyway, but in this case it was required.

Why do I mention this? It is to illustrate the importance of taking a client's needs and concerns seriously. What message would it have sent about my agency if we walked in late, even by a minute or two, for a meeting about our staff being on time? If I were the client I know what my perception would be – their management can't be on time no wonder their ambulances aren't. I would then move onto the next vendor.

But how often do we as EMS providers pull our ambulances from transfers because 9-1-1 calls are the priority? We then send an ambulance "as soon as we can" – provided another 9-1-1 call does not trump the transfer yet again. Is it any wonder why facilities we do business with get frustrated? But hold on you say, we can't let a chest pain or difficulty breathing call wait. You are correct. And I agree that occasionally pushing back a transfer because it is a lower priority in the grand scheme of things is both reasonable and prudent. But if you must do it then it is vital the facility be notified immediately. In some cases you may need to turn the call over to a competitor who can get there on time.

A client with whom you have a good rapport will understand being late once in a while. Much like employees going to work an occasional tardy can and is overlooked, but when it happens regularly for a sustained period of time there are usually consequences.

How many times does your organization allow employees to be late before discipline? Before termination occurs?

Consider this...somewhere along the line we in EMS established 90% as the acceptable level for OTP, both in the 9-1-1 world and the transfer world alike. If a staff member works 3 shifts a week and takes 2 weeks off each year 90% would allow them to be late 15 times. If they work a 5 day a week schedule, 90% would be 25 tardy occurrences a year. Is this acceptable to you? How about to your organization? If the answer is no, then why is it OK for your clients? If the answer is yes, then your organization may be in need of a culture shift toward greater accountability before OTP can be effectively addressed.

A facility calls and schedules a patient to be taken home tomorrow at 2pm. They patient is excited at the prospect. The family makes the necessary arrangements, which often includes one or more of them rearranging their work or social schedule. The facility begins the discharge process. In short, the wheels are in motion.

It is now 1:15 pm on the day of the transfer and your dispatcher has no units to send for the transfer. Now what? Hopefully they at least notify the client that they are running late. But what happens on the other end of the call? Staff had everything ready. Family, who took time off from work, was there to follow you home with the patient. What about housekeeping? They can't prep the room for the next patient. What if that next patient was in the ER and now can't be moved to their room? Now we have a delay in the ER for our incoming emergency units in dropping off their patients because beds in the ER are still full with patients waiting for their rooms on a floor who are waiting for our ambulances to come take them home.

Now our crews are frustrated by the delay, which causes them to spend more time in the ER, which causes less units available for 9-1-1 calls, which causes late responses, which causes poor patient outcomes, which causes crews to get out late...need I go on? Reality-check here folks! While we are busy bad-mouthing the facility because they can't take our patients in the ER the fact is that sometimes we are the cause of our own frustration. And when I say we, I do not mean our hardworking staff, I mean we as EMS leaders.

Hospitals are graded by Hospital Consumer Assessment of Healthcare Providers and Systems (HCAPS). One area of the survey involves the discharge process. As such, they are graded in part by our OTP and other aspects of the transfer (courtesy, professionalism, etc.). So not only do we wreak havoc on their day when we are late, we also have the potential to pull down their HCAPS. On the flip side, if we hit the mark with OTP regularly the patients win, the hospital wins, and the EMS agency can continue to flourish as their preferred or sole provider.

What can EMS agencies do to improve transfer OTP? I would say start with deployment. Be sure your staff, (dispatch and field alike, have the resources needed to get the job done. Then be sure everyone understands the importance and both human and inter-agency impact of being late vs. being on-time. Finally, create and reinforce a culture that embraces customer service and does not diminish the importance or need for non-emergency transfers.

Some specific ideas I have both seen and used myself include having hospital liaisons at larger facilities; having a staff member (EMT or Paramedic) available and stationed at a facility to assist in prepping patients for transfer; using electronic/web based scheduling applications to save time on both ends of the process; and even partnering with a facility to have your staff punch in a code on the phone in the patient's room so that housekeeping and others can immediately begin the process of prepping it for the next patient.

While some of the suggestions may have a larger financial impact than others, some will have little or no cost. That said, sometimes quality costs a little more. Ask yourself will I keep this client if I continue to provide poor OTP? The answer is obvious. Now the focus needs to be on how much is keeping their business worth? If an organization is not prepared to provide the service a client wants that organization needs to be prepared to lose that client and suffer the consequences.

If that habitually tardy employee did not take steps to invest in getting to work on time, even after you spoke with them, wouldn't you look for someone who would? A goose and gander reference comes to mind here.

# 10  9-1-1 OTP

On-time performance (OTP) is both a measure of quality and a perception factor for the public who consume our services.  If we have an extended response time only once in every 100 calls we would objectively be considering that great customer service as it relates to timeliness.  But to the one person who had to wait longer for an ambulance to arrive that same 99% OTP would have a different feel.

So what is a reasonable and appropriate response time for your area?  What is an acceptable percentage of calls that we should be there within that time frame?  These are questions that have been raised for years and will continue to be raised for years to come.  To me, no matter the answer the important thing is to hit your mark.

I had a boss a while back who put up a sign that read "Good enough is not enough and is certainly no substitute for the best."  Not sure if it was a mantra he came up with or something he found somewhere, embraced its concepts, and shared with us. No matter the origin, the sentiment is valid, especially when it comes to one aspect of 9-1-1 OTP – exceptions.

Many, if not most 9-1-1 contracts set a response time standard of number of minutes a certain percentage of the time. For example, a response time of 8:59 90% of the time. So what about the outliers? Does your agency look at them as "service failures" or not pay them much mind because they fell within the contractually allowable "margin of error"? In my view, while allowable by contract they are still "service failures". Overall the customers of the measurement period (day, week, month, year) who were provided with the agreed upon 90% OTP received "good enough" service. But what about the customers who were among the outliers? They certainly did not get "the best" service. In fact, by our own standards they didn't even receive "good enough" service.

Looking at these outliers for opportunities is a great place to start. You will find system issues and individual issues alike. The key is to investigate for cause, not blame. Often times in order to fix what happened we need to understand why it happened. We should not wait for a complaint or a survey before we look at an extended response to see what happened. Every time we do, we give away a chance to provide better customer service the next time.

These same contracts often include exceptions for a variety of things like severe weather, road construction, and spikes in call volume to name a few. To me these exceptions are intended to allow for those unusual occurrences outside an agency's control. Over time however many agencies avail themselves of these exceptions month in and month out to make the required percentage. Some argue that they are within the contract, which they are. But again, what about the customer who received an extended response we simply wrote off as an "exception"? Effectively they drew the short straw and our approach was "so what".

To me an agency should be making their marks consistently without exceptions. You committed to something, now you must make it happen. That's not to say exceptions should not be allowed, because clearly they have their place. But they are called exceptions for a reason. With exceptions is good enough to meet the minimum requirements of your contract. Hitting your targets without them should be the goal. A goal that will establish your organization among the best.

# 11 SERVICE EXCELLENCE METRICS

So what are service excellence metrics? Well they can be things like on-time performance (OTP), number of compliments, number of complaints or critical failures (like mechanical break-downs) just to name a few. There are some that are more universal and some that may be more unique to an agency's specific mission or a specific service contract. No matter what they are, it is important to identify them, measure them, and monitor performance. Doing so allows agency leaders to tout success and address opportunities for improvement promptly.

Just as we discussed the perceptions of the public and other consumers of our service earlier it is important to realize that we too can sometimes be blinded by our perceptions as well. Meaning that we all have pride in our organizations and believe we are doing well. Frankly most of us are. But the reality is that we may have a self-aggrandizing view of what we do from time to time. This is reinforced by Mark Aesch (2011) who wrote that an unspoken hostility exists toward objective measurements. His observations were that leaders didn't want executive opinion overruled by inconvenient fact. His passage reminds us that on-balance objective measurements have their place. To me, they either validate what we believe to be true or show us where what we believe might not be the case.

By listening to our customers we are engaged on the human level. But by tracking and trending we often notice things before we even know what is causing them. Tracking and trending raises the flag for us, next we must determine the cause of the unusual trend. We need to blend the data with our executive expertise (not opinion as Aesch discussed) to determine the meaning of the data. Finally, we need to decide what action should be taken.

I remember working on an OTP project. We had just taken on a new contract and needed 90% OTP to meet standards and 95% to exceed. We rose to 92% and were stuck there for two months. We hit the "good enough" standard discussed earlier, but we certainly were not doing our "best". We then did all the conventional things. We looked at deployment, at posting, at dispatcher performance, at crew chute times, and a whole lot more. The result – a lot of pertinent negatives, but no root cause was found. Was this a lot of wasted time? I say no. It was a systematic approach to rule out the more common things that cause late ambulance responses.

Was 92% the best we could do? If so, we could just monitor it and make sure it doesn't slip. No harm, no foul we are meeting standards aren't we? It gnawed at us for another month and left us with another 92% on the scorecard. Some would use the third month to validate success. To a point it would be a reasonable decision -performance had stabilized above the line – move onto the next challenge.

But we kept thinking about it and one day we noticed a different trend. On Monday and Friday afternoons we had a higher instance of crews getting out late. This was a metric we used to make sure we were taking care of our staff to get them out on time as much as is possible in EMS. It also allowed us to keep an eye on our unscheduled overtime (OT). In this case it gave us some added value. We wondered why it was mostly those two days and not others that had the increase.

When we looked we found that our time on task (TOT) – a measure of how long each call takes to complete – was significantly higher on Monday and Friday afternoons. Likely the result of some cyclical traffic patterns on the one main highway through the area. Not something we could control, but definitely something we might be able to adjust for. Because our TOT was higher we had less effective unit hours available. This snowballed into late pick-ups because the crews were not finished with one call before the next was ready. We moved around some underutilized unit hours, spread out scheduled trips a bit at call intake, and set-up a supervisor scramble unit to jump in the mix when needed. With some creativity and occasional extra effort by our supervisors and FTO's we continued our climb to 95%.

This case shows us the importance of monitoring key indicators and then applying expert analysis to them for best results. From my experience I have found that straight data could lead you astray. So too can straight opinion, conjecture, or whatever else you may want to call it. In the final analysis, both are needed to make informed and valid decisions that will improve and sustain superior performance. So don't be blinded by the numbers, but don't ignore or down play them either. Blend them into your system with an appropriate helping of critical thinking and you will be inspired by the results that can be achieved.

# 12 PERCEPTION – A CASE STUDY

A call comes in for a cardiac arrest at a local nursing facility. The call is promptly screened, and the closest ALS ambulance is dispatched. An on-duty supervisor is on the road, hears the call and knows he is in close proximity. He too responds.

A minute or two later the supervisor arrives on scene. He grabs his gear from the supervisor vehicle and proceeds inside. In spite of his almost immediate arrival he is met with a scowl. The staff abrasively challenges him on where his partner is and why he didn't have the stretcher with him.

Perception – quick response of "first responder supervisor" was meaningless because the staff thought he and his partner were being lazy because only one of them came in and they didn't bring the stretcher.

The supervisor quickly defused the situation with a concise explanation of his response and the fact that the ambulance was just a few minutes behind him. He proceeded to the patient's side, initiated care, and worked with staff and the ensuing crew to manage and transport the patient.

Why might the staff have had such a perception is the question? Could it be because in most cases when they need an ambulance it is for those "routine" transfers? Since they frequently see ambulance crews come in together with a stretcher and equipment it is likely that they have become accustomed to that as the "norm". So, when they had a critical emergency and the EMS response was different than expected they immediately bristled.

They don't fully understand how EMS works, nor should we expect them to. Sure we can do community education and such to improve understanding a bit. But ultimately we need to accept the fact that our profession, not unlike all the others, is not going to be fully understood by everyone. As such, we must be proactive in our education efforts. We also need to be ready to react calmly and professionally, as the supervisor did in this case, to defuse misunderstandings when they happen.

I enjoyed talking with the supervisor about this case. A case that did not generate a complaint, in large part I believe because of how the supervisor adeptly managed the situation. We joked that next time we had an emergency call to the same facility and a supervisor wasn't available that the crew will be questioned why a supervisor didn't respond. The supervisor did such a good job defusing he situation he may have also reset their expectations regarding a supervisor response on critical calls.

And so goes the challenges of EMS. Not just managing patients and their ailments, but also the perceptions of the people outside our industry that we encounter every day.

The best analogy I can come up with is that we are the heart and the people around us are a 12 lead. They look at us from different perspectives with a focus on what is important to them from their view. Unlike a 12-lead however, we don't always know what specifically each person's view may be. We don't know what filters their life experience will put over the lens through which they view us. They may have had a good experience, a bad one, or none whatsoever with EMS before our next encounter with them. My best advice is the old "golden rule" approach with a caveat. The caveat being that our "golden rule" may be sub-par through their "platinum lens" of $21^{st}$ century expectations. In short, do the right thing every day and be prepared to adapt and go the extra mile when necessary.

# 13 VERBILIZATION – NOT JUST FOR TESTING ANYMORE

A parent comes into the office one morning. Her concern was that "the paramedic ignored my child all the way to the hospital".

I sat with her and asked her to explain what happened.

She said her child had been sick for a couple of days. She said he woke up coughing and it scared her so she called 9-1-1. The crew arrived, found the patient to be stable and reassured her with their findings. She said she felt better at that point, but that it all changed in the back of the ambulance.

Her son was on the stretcher sitting up. She was sitting alongside the paramedic on the bench. As the ambulance started moving the boy started crying and was visibly upset. After a few attempts to calm and reassure him the medic got up and sat in the seat behind the stretcher. She felt that the paramedic just ignored her child for the rest of the ride to the hospital.

What do you think happened?

I asked her "If the paramedic had said that he was going to move because he thought his sitting so close to her son was scaring him and that he could effectively monitor him from the other seat just as easily as from where he was would that have made a difference? Her reply was simple but profound. She said "If he had done that you and I would never have met." Meaning had he done so she would have been completely satisfied with his care of her child. As a result she would not have felt the need to come in and express her dissatisfaction.

I apologized for not meeting her expectations. Even if we did everything "right" by our "protocols & procedures", we still missed the mark in her eyes. I thanked her for coming in and assured her that we would use this as a "teachable moment" for the paramedic and his partner.

Verbalization is something we have all done during testing simulations. Clearly we know how to do it, so why not use this "collateral" skill we developed in the classroom and apply it as needed when we encounter our actual patients?

This case further reinforces for us that while we often focus on outcomes that patients (and in this case their family) judge quality by their perceptions. Given this mismatch is there any wonder that we in EMS often miss the mark on customer satisfaction?

## 14 THE TOE TRUCK

So I get a call one day in my office. As I answer the phone I am met with irate screaming. After a few minutes the caller has vented sufficiently to allow us to have a conversation. She explains to me that her child had cut his foot. She said that after multiple attempts to control the bleeding herself she called 9-1-1. So far sounds reasonable, but why is she so irate just a couple of hours after the call?

The crew responded, assessed, and bandaged the foot. She told me that initially they were polite and professional enough. In fact, she even complimented them on how well they explained that even though it was a small cut, it appeared deep and would likely need a handful of stitches and a good cleaning in the hospital to properly heal. OK, now I am thinking what was all the screaming and hostility about a few minutes ago?

Well, here comes the punch line. She informed me her annoyance was about a comment they made as they were taking the child to the ambulance. Apparently, with her a few steps behind one said to the other "This lady didn't need an ambulance, she needed a toe truck" (not a typo – they did not mean a tow truck they meant toe because of the injury). So imagine my emotions. Annoyed and entertained at the same time.

Annoyed because this is EMS Humor 101 and there is no way she misunderstood the pun or made it up. I was also entertained because it is a creative and humorous pun. But there is a time and a place for everything. The reality is that making wisecracks is a common method for blowing off stress in EMS. We all do it. Just don't do it in public (Dernocoeur, 1996). We in EMS are taught to quickly assess, process, and act. Most times those skills serve us well, but every so often we slip over the line. This was a great example of the later. Lesson – be sure to check your "filter" with the rest of your equipment at the start of each shift.

As follow-up to the complaint the mom appreciated my listening and accepted our apology. I also had the crew stop by my office – just a few hours after the call. When they knocked, I looked up and said "A toe truck huh? They both immediately dropped their heads and apologized. We sat and talked about it for a few minutes and turned it into a positive. I have shared the story many, many times and have now included it in this book. In the end the toe truck has gotten some great positive mileage in the years since its inappropriate maiden voyage.

# 15 BRIDGE TROLLS
# & NEGATIVE INFLUENCES

In the October 2005 edition of *JEMS Magazine* Thom Dick reviewed a couple of books by a paramedic who tells stories of his experiences in EMS. In it Thom says that the author "writes with all the enlightenment and sophistication of a bridge troll".

Given Thom's reputation for the positive, including his book *People Care* and the fact that I knew and worked for the same organization as the author he refers to as a "bridge troll" I had some serious concerns. Having not read his books before Thom's reviews I got myself copies. At first I was a bit miffed at the fact dozens of his coworkers and mine were listed in the acknowledgements and I was not among them. But when I read some of the stories I was glad I wasn't. I also saw some of the things that had Thom so fired up.

There were stories of flat out disrespect for other human beings and even, in my view admissions of assault. One particularly disturbing story was about a patient who had overdosed. As one crew member was administering Narcan his role was to "set the scene". He relates the story like this...

> "We turned off the lights in the back of the truck, except for the medic's MagLite. I put three inch tape across his eye brows. When he started to stir like the Narcan was kicking in, I yanked the tape off his eyes. He woke up screaming. The medic leaned over him with the flashlight on his face and vampire fangs in his mouth and began hissing. The patient screamed again and let loose his bowels once more" (Kerins, 2004).

In some respects I guess I am glad I didn't work with Devin much. That said, my first tour chief who later went on to become the EMS Director had a mantra of "what you permit, you promote". Since Devin didn't pull this sort of thing when he worked with me and didn't include me in his acknowledgements I guess maybe he knew better, at least around me.

As EMS providers we are entrusted with the lives of strangers at perhaps their most vulnerable of times. It is a lot of responsibility that must be taken seriously. Before we even begin to engage in our clinical skills we need to provide respect and dignity to every human being we encounter. The flurry of activity at an emergency scene can strip a person of these things astonishingly fast (Dernocoeur, 1996). Intentionally creating opportunities to strip a patient's dignity has no place in EMS. Think about it... How many medics do you know who carry vampire fangs as standard equipment? In my view the above story, as related shows both inappropriate (if not illegal) activity with malice of intent (Why else would an EMS provider have vampire fangs as readily available as their MagLite?).

Developing personal awareness is a continual process throughout life. It demands adjustments along the way, as we integrate new views of the world (Dernocoeur, 1996). It is my sincere hope that with about a decade behind his books and Thom Dick's blistering review that he has become a more self-aware.

While EMS enjoys a positive view in most communities we will always have work to do relative to setting and maintaining expectations. I was at a convention a few years back and while walking past the vendors I noticed a t-shirt that read "EMT – I am here to save your ass not kiss it." Well if that didn't sum it up! They had it prominently displayed and a stack of them in a variety of sizes. Clearly this was not a custom shirt for a single individual. I asked if they sold many and they said they did.

Guess what. I bought one too! No, it wasn't back when I was young and foolish. It was about 5 years ago. I have yet to wear it and never will. I bought it to use as a prop for classes and orientations. I hold it up and usually get a few chuckles initially. Then I follow it up with informing the group that if this shirt represents them then whether student or new employee they should think about leaving. Effectively I tell them that if they would be comfortable wearing the shirt that we would not be comfortable with them wearing our uniform.

You guessed it; I now have their full attention. And yes I have even had a couple of people leave their ID on the table and leave on their first day. Guess they felt more comfortable wearing the shirt than wearing what my organization's uniform stood for. For those who stay and most do I reinforce the organization's values and leverage the few minutes of undivided attention I have gained before they go back to counting the minutes until the next break.

Establishing an environment of dignity and respect is a required first step for the leaders of every EMS organization. Doing so and then following it up by walking the talk every day will go a long way toward providing outstanding customer service consistently and continually. Highly successful people believe in going the extra mile in their jobs. They do the things others are unwilling to do (Willingham, 2005). In short, model the way, don't be a character in a bridge troll story, and never wear that t-shirt.

# 16 PATCH UP YOUR HOUSE

The title of this chapter sounds more like a job for Bob Vela of *This Old House* fame or perhaps the name a new TV Reality show. But it's actually my view of what we need to do in EMS as a way of becoming more well-rounded providers of patient care.

The movie *Patch Adams* is based on a real doctor whose approach was to connect with his patients as people. It was a great movie, one which I believe every EMS provider should watch as part of their initial and refresher training alike.

On the flip side is the television series *House*. This show centered around a cynical diagnostician whose focus was on solving the puzzles that were his patient's medical conditions. He spent little time getting to know his patients and lived by the mantra of "everybody lies". That said - his relentless pursuit of finding the cause and the cure was admirable.

Interestingly, but telling just the same is the fact that *Patch Adams* got a movie and *House* got an eight season run in prime time and now appears often on cable and satellite TV. Why is that I wonder? Could it be because even though he is a fictional character Dr.

House is more in line with the public's experiences with medical care? A cynical character draws better ratings from a cynical audience and there are more cynics than optimists out there today perhaps?

No matter the reason, the message I would like to put forth is that we need to be clinically competent for sure, but no matter the severity of our patients' conditions they are all people first. Patch shows us the importance of the human connection.

There is a scene in the movie where Patch Adams is doing rounds with his fellow residents and the attending physician. They stop at the side of a woman on a stretcher in the hallway. She is dressed in nothing but a hospital gown. The attending begins to ramble on about her condition and symptoms. She looks very uncomfortable and perhaps a bit embarrassed. Patch then asks "What's the patient's name?" The attending answers with a scowl "Margarie." Patch then says "Hello Margarie." She smiles and the attending simply says "Let's move on".

What did Margarie need and what did she get? She needed Patch's empathy as well as the discussion of her condition. But she needed it in a different order, a different way. Perhaps even an attempt to find out why this patient was in the hallway and not in a room so that her privacy could be addressed. And I am not just talking HIPAA here. Think how you would feel if you or a loved one were lying in a hallway alone and about an inch away from naked for everyone to see. Would that be OK? I hope you answered no.

Dr. House is very much like the attending in *Patch Adams*. He only spoke to patients when he had to and most times they were not pleasant interpersonal exchanges. I think he left as many patients and their families upset - even angry at some point during their stay as he cured. There were some episodes however where he seemed to get the people part. These episodes showed he had the capacity to do so, but opted for cynical obnoxious puzzle solver more. It was likely because he had somehow become more comfortable in that role than he was with the more interpersonal approach.

Here are my questions for your consideration. Have many in EMS become more House than Patch? Has this occurred because following objective protocols is easier than the subjectivity of the more interpersonal human connection? How much is the provider's fault and how much falls on leadership?

Consider this, in his book *If Disney Ran Your Hospital* Fred Lee (2004) suggests that people don't do what their organizations (or the public) expect. They do what their mangers pay attention to. I recall vividly a conversation I had with someone I worked with. His philosophy was as simple as it was profound. He said "Everything is a leadership issue."

So if we in EMS leadership and management roles are focusing too much on objective outcomes and spending little time on the interpersonal aspects of our operations are we to blame? I think the answer to this one is yes. Don't get me wrong, the old adage of "you can't manage what you don't measure" still applies, but it needs to be tempered with a focus on people.

Easier said than done? Absolutely! But that doesn't mean we can't do it.

# 17 HE'S MY DAD

The following was adapted to EMS from an anonymous letter sent to a healthcare organization by the daughter of a patient. Its intent in this context is to allow us to walk a mile in the shoes of a family member and in so doing gain some perspective we may not otherwise have. I originally received a copy of a copy of the original may years back. Don't remember who first gave me a copy, but do I recall how moved I was by its content.

As you read the letter consider this…

"Too often we underestimate the power of a touch, a smile, a kind word, a listening ear, an honest compliment, or the smallest act of caring, all of which have the potential to turn a life around."

-Leo Buscaglia (as cited in Michelli, 2007)

-

To each staff member of this organization:

As you respond to your next call I hope you will remember what I am about to say.

I spent part of yesterday with you. I was there with my mother and father. We didn't know what we were supposed to do, for we had never needed your services before.

I watched yesterday as my dad became a puzzle to solve, a diagnosis to put on your chart, a case number, a task that needed to be completed before you could go back to your station and watch TV.

I saw a weak man shuffled through a system of impatient EMS workers, a burned-out nursing staff, and a budget-scarce hospital, being robbed of any dignity and pride he may have had left. I was amazed at how impersonal your staff was, huffing and blowing when the patient (my dad) did not give you the answer to your question that you were looking for or when one of us family members asked a question to make some sense of our fear of the unknown.

My dad is only a file number to clutter your day, a patient who will ask questions again after they have been mechanically answered the first time. But no, that's not really my dad. That's only what you see.

What you don't see is a cabinet maker since the age of 14, a self-employed man who has a wonderful wife, four grown kids (who visit too much), and five grandchildren (with two more on the way) – all of whom think their "pop" is the greatest. This man is everything a daddy should be – strong and firm, yet tender; rough around the edges; a country boy, yet respected by prominent business owners.

He's my dad, the man who raised me through thick and thin, gave me away as a bride, held my children at their births, stuffed a $20 bill into my hand when times were tough and comforted me when I cried. Now we are told that before long cancer will take this man away from us.

You may say that these are the words of a grieving daughter lashing out in helplessness at the prospect of losing a loved one. I would not disagree. Yet I would urge you not to discount what I say. **NEVER LOSE SIGHT OF THE PEOPLE BEHIND YOUR CALLS. EACH CALL REPRESENTS A PERSON** – with feeling, a history, a life – whom you have the power to touch one day by your words, actions, and attitudes. Tomorrow it may be your loved one – your relative or neighbor – who turns into a case number, a task to be marked off before you move onto your next call or the end of your shift.

I hope that you will reward the next person you greet on a call with a kind word and a smile because that person is someone's dad, husband, wife, mother, son or daughter – or simply because he or she is a human being deserving of the same respect and dignity you would expect if the roles were reversed.

*-Anonymous*

In the final analysis, many of the major problems of quality revolve around customer service and process quality rather than the question of whether the vast majority of patients go home with excellent clinical and scientific outcomes (Lathrop, 1993). Looking at this "letter" I see too much House, not enough Patch. I see an atmosphere in dire need of leadership at all levels. How about you?

I have since found in my research for this project that the original version was published in one of the *Chicken Soup for the Soul* books. I find it great to see it being so widely shared. I also wonder if the original author has any idea what a significant and continuing impact she has had on the people in healthcare fortunate enough to have read it. I bet her dad would be proud!

# 18 INVEST IN CUSTOMER SERVICE

Like most EMS agencies, yours probably has a mission statement, a vision, and a set of values. Bet they look great on the posters around your stations and on your letterheads and e-mail signatures too! But do they have meaning, real meaning to your front line people? When it comes to communicating with the customer no one is more important than these point-of-encounter employees (Nykiel, 1990). As a result it is imperative that EMS leaders invest in them. And invest beyond the required items like uniforms, health insurance, and clinical continuing education.

Does anyone reading this recall the section on customer service in your EMT or Paramedic training? Some may recall a lecture on communications or even have the privilege of learning from an instructor who baked-in customer service at certain points in the class. But by and large the answer is probably no. Why? Because it is not a part of the curriculum and we need to stick to the curriculum. The result – well trained clinicians with very little education in taking care of the customer as a person. We teach them to be House and pay very little attention to what Patch brings to the table.

I remember a weekend a few years back. I was on my way someplace and had my two dogs in the back seat. I made a quick stop at a Burger King for a breakfast sandwich and a cup of coffee. I placed my order at the first window and as I pulled up to the second I heard the manager call out for two strips of bacon. I didn't think anything of it at the time, but when he came to my window with my order and asked if he could give my dogs a treat it made an impression. Was that something Burger King taught him? Another company he previously worked for perhaps? Or was he just a natural? Not sure of the answers to any of these questions but, as Bell & Bell (2003) put it, he created a magnetic service miracle. His extra mile gesture left me with a very positive feeling about him and Burger King. He left me eager to tell the story to others whenever the subject of customer service came up.

Sure some have a natural talent for interpersonal skills, but many, if not most of us would benefit from some affective education on the topic. And with all the mediums out there for education – classroom, on-line, sim-labs, and others – one would think this would be an easy task. But I assure you it is not.

Not trying to discourage you from the very thing I am suggesting in this chapter – just setting the difficulty scale for you. Think of the pain scale and consider this... CPR Refresher might be a 1; a 12 Lead EKG class might hit a 5; and Customer Service Training would be around a 9 or 10. That's a 9 or 10 in difficulty, but the pain need not be equal. In fact, the more you do it and the better you get at it the less difficult and painful it will become.

If your agency does not have customer service training in place already this will involve change. Even if it does and you seek to update it – change. Think about some of your previous change projects. One that comes to mind for me is the transition from paper PCR's to electronic. What we learned in this and many other projects is that any form of change may be difficult to communicate and the difficulty can be compounded when the change involves behavior (Nykiel, 1990). Change evokes a host of emotions. But it also creates energy, both positive and negative. Organizations and their leaders that can harness that energy have far more success than those who ignore it or allow it to derail the project.

Making an organization's mission, vision, and values come alive and jump off the page requires a top to bottom commitment. It requires training, both initial and on-going for everyone in the organization. It requires a daily focus on the details that matter. There is no one resource for any of the components of an effective customer service atmosphere. Perception is reality for all humans. Our challenge is finding a formula for our organization that makes our mission, visions, and values real – not just words on a page. When we accomplish this we will have aligned perception and reality. They will become synonyms.

# 19 NICE MATTERS

A coworker has a sign in her office and it simply says "Nice Matters". If handled properly in most organizations that sign could probably replace pages and pages of policies and procedures with positive results. It is what life is all about and definitely should be central to what EMS is all about.

When we respond to a call the expectation of the caller is that we will fix their problem. But there is more to it than that. We need to be nice about it, even if it is something that might not have warranted an ambulance response from a purely clinical perspective.

In EMS we are often dealing with people at their most vulnerable. We need to not only fix their ailment, we need to connect with them and help them navigate the situation.

> Anyone who has ever know the frustration of calling a "customer service" phone line only to be sent on an endless loop of transfers by some mindless machine, knows the value of speaking to a real person about real problems (Molitor, 2007).

We are concerned with their breathing and so are they. But they are also concerned about multiple bags of perishable groceries they were bringing in when they started to get short of breath and call us. Is there something we can do about the groceries? I would say sometimes yes and sometimes no, but I would never say unequivocally it was not our job. If it is just my partner and I and the patient is critical then the groceries might be on their own. But if we had an extra rider or there were first responders, police, or others on scene that could take on that task without delaying or compromising patient care I believe it is 100% something we can and should take responsibility for. Doing so shows compassion and will help put their mind at ease while they recover from their medical condition.

As EMS providers we are considered leaders in our communities. In this role it is important that we understand refining our human reactions and capabilities increase our emotional intelligence. The effective use of this increased/improved emotional intelligence creates the capability to lead in a human way that reflects kindness, consideration, respect, and patience (Brunacini & Brunacini, 2005). Applying these four elements to every interaction we have with patients, their families, and the public at large is essential to our success in EMS.

For those reading this with a fire service background it is probably a safe bet that you have heard of Alan Brunacini. For those who don't, he was the Chief of the

Phoenix Arizona Fire Department. Among his many contributions to emergency services was his belief in customer service. In fact he even had "be nice" painted on fire apparatus along with the department logo. One of the best examples of customer service in the Brunacini led Phoenix Fire Department was a response they had for a man having chest pain. The response was an ALS Engine and an ambulance. They treated the patient and loaded him into the ambulance. The crew of the Engine then took a few minutes to finish the already poured concrete slab before it hardened in a less than desirable state. I am not saying we need to be jacks of all trades, but in this case the Engine crew knew how to do the work and prevented a problem from occurring.

Granted the folks in Phoenix were empowered by their Renaissance Chief. So I guess my question is this - How empowered do your leaders allow you to be?

To me, no matter the nature of the call nice is required. In fact nice often defuses an otherwise potentially difficult situation as often as not being nice (or being perceived as such) inflames an otherwise calm situation. Nice is not only the right thing to do, it often keeps people safe! Also, going the extra mile, within reason and capability, is what I consider value added service. Strive to do it as often as you can.

# 20 ESSENTIALS OF CUSTOMER SERVICE IN EMS

I leave you with the following 12 Essentials of Customer Service:

1. Always be nice, it's a force multiplier.
2. There is a huge difference between not knowing and not caring.
3. Say please and thank you even when it is a matter of life and death.
4. Wipe your feet at the door.
5. Tell your patients that it was a pleasure to meet them and an honor to be of service and mean it.
6. Iron your uniform, polish your shoes and wash your ambulance.
7. Your patient is not named, honey, babe, sweetie, darling, bud, pal, man, or hey.  Use your patient's name when speaking with them.  Sir and Ma'am are acceptable alternatives.
8. You are always on camera.  Act like it.
9. Emergency services were never about you.
10. People always remember how you make them feel.
11. You can never truly know the full extent of your influence.

12. Service is at the heart of everything we do. The farther away from that concept you drift the more you are likely to become lost.

Adapted from 101 Things We Should Teach Every New EMT. Check it out on www.theemtspot.com where this list of pearls for EMS continues to grow.

# REFERENCES AND RESOURCES

Adams, P. & Mylander, M. (2008). *Gesundheit*. Rochester Vermont. Healing Arts Press.

Administrator. The EMT Spot. *101 Things We Should Teach Every EMT*. Retrieved 1/18/2015 from http://theemtspot.com/2014/03/22/101-things-we-should-teach-every-new-emt/

Aesch, M. (2011). *Driving Excellence - Transform Your Organization's Culture and Achieve Revolutionary Results*. New York, New York. Hyperion Books.

Bell, C. R. & Bell, B. (2003). *Magnetic Service - Secrets for Creating Passionately Devoted Customers*. San Francisco. Berrett-Koehler Publishers, Inc.

Brunacini, A.V. & Brunacini, N. (2005). *The Anatomy and Physiology of Leadership*. Peoria, Arizona. Uptown Graphics & Design.

Dernocoeur, K. B. (1996). *Streetsense - Communication, Safety, and Control*. Redmond, WA. Laing Research Services.

Dick, T. (2005). Not a Bus Driver? Don't Waste Your Money on These Two Books. Jems. October 2005.

Dick, T. (2005). *People Care*. Van Nuys, CA. Cygnus Business Media.

Gorman, L. (2006). *L.L. Bean - The Making of an American Icon*. Boston, Massachusetts. Harvard Business School Press.

Kazanjian, K. (2013). *Driving Loyalty - Turning Every Customer and Employee into a Raving Fan for Your Brand*. New York. Crown Business.

Kerins, D. (2004). *EMS 2 - The Life of Your Job*. Poughkeepsie, NY. ViviSphere Publishing.

Lathrop, J. P. (1993). *Restructuring Healthcare - The Patient Focused Paradigm*. San Francisco, CA. Jossey-Bass.

Lee, F. (2004). *If Disney Ran Your Hospital*. Bozeman, MT. Second River Healthcare Press.

LL Bean Guarantee Retrieved from http://www.llbean.com/customerService/aboutLLBean/guarantee.html on 12/20/2014.

Lynch, R. L. & Cross, K. F. (1994). *Measure Up! Yardsticks for Continuous Improvement*. Cambridge MA. Blackwell Publishers.

Michelli, J. A. (2007). *The Starbucks Experience*. New York, NY. McGraw Hill.

Molitor, B. D. (2007). *Win Win Win*. United States of America. Authentic Publishing.

Moran, T. L. (Producer). (2004). *House, M.D.* [Television Series].  [With hugh Laurie, Lisa Edelstein, Omar Epps, Robert Sean Leonard, Jennifer Morrison, Jesse Spencer, Peter Jacobson, Kal Penn, Olivia Wilde, Amber Tamblyn, Odette Annable, and Charlyne Yi].  United States.  NBC Universal Television Studio.

Nykiel, R. A. (1990). *You Can't Lose if the Customer Wins - Ten Steps to Service Success*.  United States of America.  Longmeadow Press.

Performance Research Associates, Applegate, T. & Applegate, J. (2009).  *101 Activities for Delivering Knock Your Socks off Service.*  New York, NY.  American Management Association.

Peters, T. J. & Waterman, R. H. (2004) *In Search of Excellence - Lessons from America's Best-Run Companies*.  New York, NY. MJF Books.

Shadyac, T. (Director). (1998). *Patch Adams.* [Motion Picture]. [With  Robin Williams, Monica Potter, Philip Seymour Hoffman and Bob Gunton].  United States.  Universal Pictures.

Snow, D. & Yankovitch, T. (2003). *Unleashing Excellence - The Complete Guide to Ultimate Customer Service*.  Sanford Florida.  D C Press.

Willingham, R. (1992). *Hey, I'm the Customer.* New York, New York.  Prentice Hall.

Willingham, R. (2005). *Integrity Service - Treat Your Customers Right Watch Your Business Grow.* New York, New York. Free Press.

Yellen, Emily (2009). *Your Call is Not That Important to Us.* New York, New York. Free Press.

Zemke, R. & Bell, C. (2003). *Service Magic - The Art of Amazing Your Customers.* United States of America. Dearborn Trade Publishing.


Cover Photo: www.dreamstime.com

# ABOUT THE AUTHOR

John R. Brophy has been in EMS for over 30 years. He has held provider and leadership roles in both operations and communications. His diverse experience and story-telling ability have positioned him as a frequent speaker at national and regional conferences. Over the years he has published numerous trade journal articles. This book is his fifth on a variety of EMS and leadership topics.

# OTHER TITLES BY JOHN R. BROPHY

Leadership Essentials for Emergency Medical Services

21$^{st}$ Century Leadership

Reflections – A Leadership Anthology

Dynamic Deployment – A Primer for EMS (co-written with Dale Loberger)

www.ingramcontent.com/pod-product-compliance
Lightning Source LLC
Chambersburg PA
CBHW051729170526
45167CB00002B/864